KUMON READING WORKBOOKS

Reading

Table of Contents

KUMON

Vocabulary Review

Date / /   Name

Score
/100

1 Trace each word below. Then read it aloud.

8 points per question

(1) block

(2) clap

(3) flag

(4) plug

(5) frog

2 Complete the words using the letters from the box below.

2 points per question

| fl | cl | br | cr | gr | pl |

(1)  | g | r | a | s | s |

(2) | p | l | a | y |

(3)  | b | r | a | g |

(4) 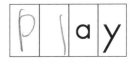 | c | r | a | b |

(5) | f | l | y |

(6) | G | l | a | s | s |

2   © Kumon Publishing Co., Ltd.

3 Connect each word to the correct picture below.

4 points per question

(1) class

(2) plane

(3) grape

(4) clean

(5) green

(6) brick

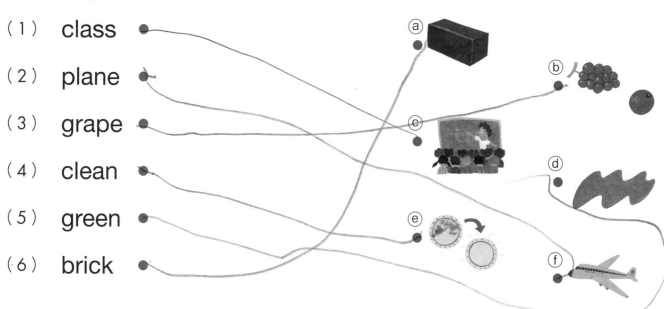

ⓐ ⓑ ⓒ ⓓ ⓔ ⓕ

4 Complete each sentence using a word from the box.

4 points per question

| block   flag   clock   class   plum   grass |

(1) Fly the _fdag_ !

(2) The _class_ will clap.

(3) I grab _brickn_ .

(4) That is a black _blok_ .

(5) I eat a _plum_ on the plane.

(6) The _clock_ is clean.

You can go to the head of the class!

Vocabulary Review

Level
Score
/100
Date / /
Name

1 Connect each word to the correct picture below.

4 points per question

(1) skate •

(2) snap •

(3) slip •

(4) glass •

(5) bike •

(6) glove •

ⓐ

ⓑ

ⓒ

ⓓ

ⓔ

ⓕ

2 Complete the words using the letters from the box below.

4 points per question

sn	sl	sk	cl	gl	sl

(1) | s | k | a | t | e |

(2) | | | a | p |

(3) | | | i | p |

(4) 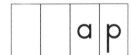 | | | a | s | s |

(5) | | | i | d | e |

(6) | | | o | v | e |

3 Complete each word below. Use the pictures as hints.

3 points per question

(1)  te _____

(2) wi _____

(3) st _____

(4) la _____

(5) dr _____

(6) pl _____

(7) te _____

(8) li _____

4 Complete each sentence using a word from the box.

7 points per question

lost	pink	rock	end

(1) I think of _____.

(2) He came in last and _____.

(3) Just a bend and then the _____.

(4) I always pack my _____.

That was a blast.

5

3

Vocabulary Review

Level

Date / /

Name

Score

/100

1 Trace each word below. Then read it aloud.

3 points per question

(1) street

(2) string

(3) stripe

(4) stream

(5) splash

(6) spray

(7) strong

(8) split

2 Circle the correct picture to match each word below.

4 points per question

(1) press

ⓐ   ⓑ

(2) spill

ⓤ    ⓑ

(3) spin

ⓐ   ⓑ

(4) step

ⓐ   ⓑ

(5) store

ⓐ    ⓑ

(6) start

ⓐ   ⓑ

3 Write the words below. Use the pictures as hints.
4 points per question

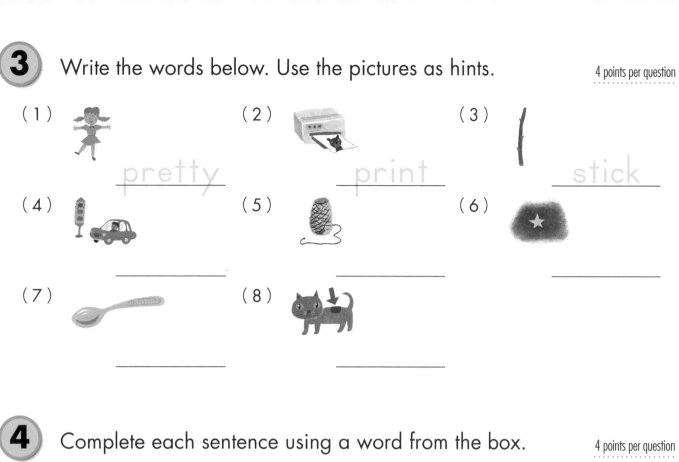

(1) _pretty_

(2) _print_

(3) _stick_

(4) _____

(5) _____

(6) _____

(7) _____

(8) _____

4 Complete each sentence using a word from the box.
4 points per question

strong　spray　splash　street　stream

(1) I will _____ you in the pool!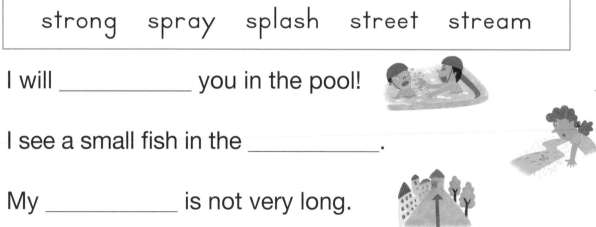

(2) I see a small fish in the _____.

(3) My _____ is not very long.

(4) Will you _____ the car with water?

(5) My dad is _____! He can lift me up in the air.

Way to go!

Vocabulary Review

Date   /   /

Name

Level ☆

Score   /100

1 Trace each word below. Then read it aloud.

3 points per question

(1) stretch

(2) scratch

(3) watch

(4) father

(5) cloth

(6) witch

(7) three

(8) mother

2 Circle the word that matches each picture.

5 points per question

(1) brother   cloth   mother   broken

(2) watch   itch   witch   when

(3) scratch   stretch   catch   sat

(4) patch   itch   watch   catch

3 Write the words below. Use the pictures as hints.

(1) witch

(2)  watch

(3) mother

(4)  cloth

(5) catch

(6) stretch

4 Finish each sentence below. Use the pictures as hints.

(1) My father asked me to clean my room.

(2) Look at my new watch .

(3) The cat gave me a scratch on my foot.

(4) It is three o'clock now.

(5) Always stretch before you run.

You can shine!

5 Vowels

Level ☆

Date / /

Name

Score /100

1 Trace each word below. Then read it aloud.

1 point per question

(1) can

(2) first

(3) fur

(4) her

(5) horn

(6) hard

(7) jar

(8) bird

(9) cart

(10) fork

2 Write the letter of the correct picture next to each word below.

30 points for completion

(1) cat (h)   car (d)   (2) hen (c)   her (g)

(3) fire (f)   first (L)   (4) hot (e)   horn (J)

(5) fun (K)   fur (a)   (6) hand (b)   hard (i)

ⓐ    ⓑ    ⓒ 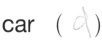   ⓓ

ⓔ 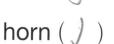   ⓕ    ⓖ    ⓗ

ⓘ    ⓙ   ⓚ    ⓛ

3 Write the words below. Use the pictures as hints.   5 points per question

(1) J ar

(2)  fork

(3)  fur

(4)  first

(5)  bird

(6)  horn

4 Complete each sentence using a word from the box.   5 points per question

bird	first	fur	fork	horn	jar

(1) I like the jelly in that _Jar_.

(2) The _bird_ flew up into the sky.

(3) Honk your _horn_.

(4) Use your _fork_, not your hands!

(5) My cat has soft _fur_.

(6) I came in _first_ in my class on the test.

You are a star!

1 Trace each word below. Then read it aloud.

4 points per question

(3) point

(1) coin

(4) soil

(2) boy

(5) toy

(6) enjoy

2 Circle the correct picture to match each word below.

4 points per question

(1) toy
ⓐ   ⓑ

(2) enjoy
ⓐ  ⓑ

(3) soil
ⓐ  ⓑ

(4) boy
ⓐ   ⓑ

(5) boil
ⓐ   ⓑ

(6) join
ⓐ ⓑ

3 Make words to match the pictures by using the puzzle pieces below.

4 points per question

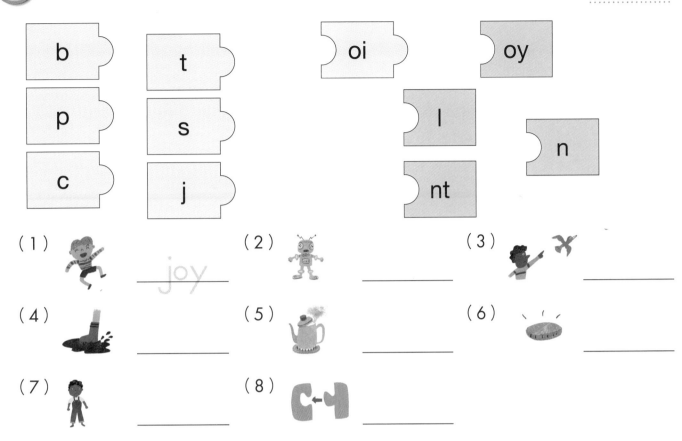

(1) _joy_

(2) _____

(3) _____

(4) _____

(5) _____

(6) _____

(7) _____

(8) _____

4 Finish each sentence below. Use the pictures as hints.

4 points per question

(1) Mom told us not to _____ at her.

(2) Dad wants to _____ water for tea.

(3) Tom lost his _____ on the way to class.

(4) I broke my _____ when I fell down.

(5) I _____ a nice, cold glass of water.

You are a joy!

13

7 Vowels

Level ★★

Date   /   /

Name

Score   /100

1 Trace each word below. Then read it aloud.

4 points per question

(1) cloud

(2) house

(3) mouth

(4) loud

(5) out

(6) round

(7) mouse

> Most of the time, **ou** makes a sound like **ou** in `out`!'

2 Trace each word below. Then read it aloud.

4 points per question

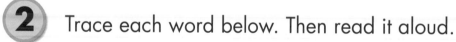

(1)   (2)   (3)

you   soup   group

> Sometimes, the **ou** makes a sound like the **ou** in `you`!'

3 Connect each word to the correct picture below.

3 points per question

(1) loud   •

(2) out   •

(3) you   •

(4) mouse •

ⓐ

ⓑ

ⓒ

ⓓ

4 Trace each word below. Then read it aloud.

(1) throw

(2) crow

(3) arrow

(4) bow

(5) tower

(6) cow

(7) down

(8) flower

5 Complete each sentence using a word from the box.

cow	arrow	tower	flower	round	crow

(1) The _____ was tall.

(2) She had a _____ ball.

(3) The _____ lay down.

(4) The _____ flew through the air.

(5) He gave his mom a _____ .

(6) The _____ landed on the house.

I'd like to live in Old Town!

1 Trace each word below. Then read it aloud.

2 points per question

(1) room

(2) tooth

(3) stool

(4) broom

(5) moon

(6) pool

(7) boot

(8) spoon

2 Connect each word to the correct picture below.

3 points per question

(1) pool •

(2) broom •

(3) moon •

(4) boot •

(5) spoon •

(6) stool •

(7) tooth •

(8) room •

ⓐ •

ⓑ •

ⓒ •

ⓓ •

ⓔ •

ⓕ •

ⓖ •

ⓗ •

3 Make words to match the pictures by using the puzzle pieces below. Write the words on the lines. You can use "oo" piece more than once.

3 points per question

f [ ] t   w [ ] d   b [ ] k

oo

l [ ] k   g [ ] d   c [ ] k

h [ ] k   t [ ] k

(1 ) _____   (2 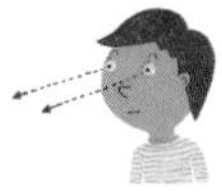) _____   (3 ) _____

(4 ) _____   (5 ) _____   (6 ) _____

(7 ) _____   (8 ) _____

4 Complete each sentence using a word from the box.

6 points per question

book	room	foot	spoon	pool	look

(1) I like to read my _____ all the time.

(2) Let's go jump in the _____.

(3) Jim hurt his _____ in the park.

(4) Do you eat your ice cream with a _____?

(5) Lana's _____ is very clean.

(6) Where is your pen? Did you _____ by your desk?

Now you are cooking!

17

1 Trace each word below. Then read it aloud.

4 points per question

(1) nice

(2) dice

(3) mice

(4) ice

(5) price

(6) rice

2 Circle the picture that matches the sentence.

6 points per question

(1) My mom is very nice.

Ⓒ   Ⓑ

(2) I like water with ice.

Ⓒ   Ⓑ

(3) The mice ran into the rice.

Ⓒ   Ⓑ

(4) The price for the dice was too much.

Ⓒ   Ⓑ

3 Trace each word below. Then read it aloud.

4 points per question

(1) flight

(2) bright

(3) right

(4) fright

(5) light

(6) night

(7) sight

4 Complete each sentence using a word from the box.

4 points per question

ice	light	nice	night	mice	right

(1) Turn _____ at the bus stop.

(2) It is too hot today. I need more _____ in my water!

(3) Turn the _____ on please. It is dark in here.

(4) It is a dark _____ and there is no moon.

(5) The _____ ate the cheese.

(6) Our teacher is very _____! She is never mean.

That was right!
What a nice job you did.

10 Consonant Combinations

Level ★★

Date   /   /

Name

Score   /100

1 Use one of the groups of letters from the box to finish each word below. Then say the word aloud.

2 points per question

| all | oll | ull | ell | ill |

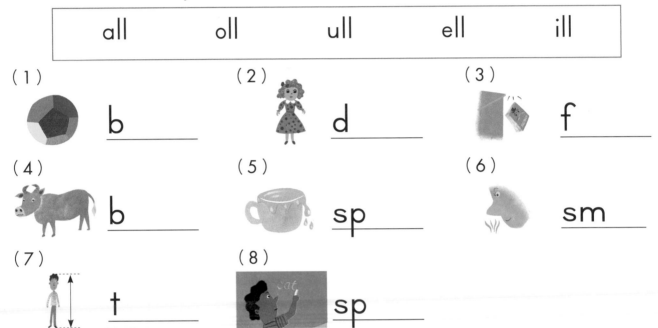

(1) b_____

(2) d_____

(3) f_____

(4) b_____

(5) sp_____

(6) sm_____

(7) t_____

(8) sp_____

2 Make words to match the pictures by using the puzzle pieces below. Write the words on the lines. You can use each piece more than once.

3 points per question

| b | k | sn | | o | i | ss |
| cl | pr | gr | | a | e | ff |

(1) off_____

(2) _____

(3) _____

(4) _____

(5) _____

(6) _____

(7) _____

(8) _____

3 Complete each word pair below. Then say both words aloud.

6 points per question

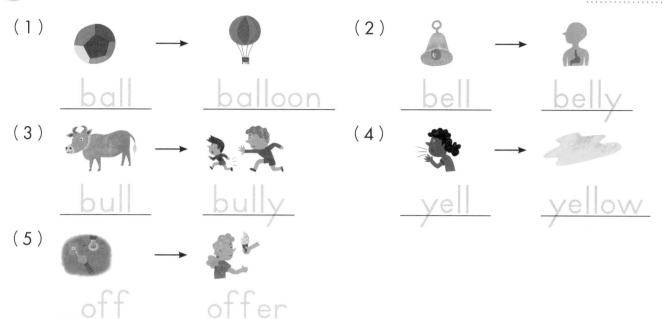

(1) ball → balloon

(2) bell → belly

(3) bull → bully

(4) yell → yellow

(5) off → offer

4 Complete each sentence using a word from the box.

5 points per question

| ball | balloon | class | sniff | off | offer |

(1) There is a test in _____ today.

(2) Jimmy kicked the _____ into the net.

(3) Mom asked if I was sick when she saw me _____.

(4) Turn the light _____. I want to sleep.

(5) Did she _____ to clean your room? How nice!

(6) Jane is sad. Her _____ flew away.

You can spell well!

Consonant Combinations

Level ☆☆

Date / /

Name

Score /100

1 Trace each word below. Then read it aloud.

2 points per question

(1)  summer

(2) hurry

(3)  tunnel

(4)  winner

(5) mirror

(6) hammer

(7) carrot

(8) parrot

2 Draw a line to match the words with the correct pictures.

3 points per question

(1) furry ●————————● ⓐ

(2) winner ●

ⓑ

(3) dinner ●

ⓒ

(4) carrot ●

ⓓ

(5) parrot ●

ⓔ

(6) swimmer ●

ⓕ

(7) hammer ●

ⓖ

(8) mirror ●

ⓗ

3 Write each word below. Use the box and the pictures as hints.

3 points per question

berry	funny	carrot	hello
tunnel	yellow	dinner	summer

(1) _____

(2) _____

(3) _____

(4) _____

(5) _____

(6) _____

(7) _____

(8) _____

4 Complete each sentence using a word from the box.

6 points per question

summer	parrot	jelly	winner	mirror	hurry

(1) It is very hot this _____. I like it!

(2) Sue is sad. Her _____ flew away.

(3) We must _____ to catch the bus.

(4) Ankur was fast and came in first.
He was the _____.

(5) I like toast with _____ in the morning.

(6) What do you see in the _____?

You are a winner!

12 Compound Words

Level ☆☆

Score

/100

Date   /   /

Name

1 Read each word. Then trace the compound words.

4 points per question

(1)
snow   man   snowman

(2)
up   hill   uphill

(3)
black   bird   blackbird

Don't forget!
A compound word is a word made from two other words.
ex. up + hill=**uphill**

2 Read the words below. Then write the letter of each picture next to the correct word below.

8 points per question

ⓐ ⓑ ⓒ ⓓ
ⓔ ⓕ ⓖ ⓗ
ⓘ ⓙ ⓚ ⓛ
ⓜ ⓝ ⓞ

(1) ① cow (h) ② boy ( ) ③ cowboy ( )

(2) ① foot ( ) ② ball ( ) ③ football ( )

(3) ① rain ( ) ② bow ( ) ③ rainbow ( )

(4) ① door ( ) ② bell ( ) ③ doorbell ( )

(5) ① dog ( ) ② house ( ) ③ doghouse ( )

3 Combine the words from the box to make compound words. Use the pictures as hints.

4 points per question

snow	cow	up	boy	rain	fire
bow	flake	grass	hopper	stairs	place

(1) _____

(2) _____

(3) _____

(4) _____

(5) _____

(6) _____

4 Complete each sentence using a word from the box.

4 points per question

shoemaker	fireplace	playground
football	lunchroom	cowboy

(1) A _shoemaker_ makes shoes.

(2) Do you want to play with me on the _____?

(3) At school, we eat our lunch in the _____.

(4) Let us get warm in front of the _____.

(5) When he plays _____, my brother wears a helmet.

(6) The _____ made his horse go fast.

You can do anything!

Compound Words

Date / /   Name

1 Read the following sentences. Underline the compound words. Then write the two words that make up the compound words. *4 points per question*

(1) We made a snowman but we did not have a carrot for the nose!

_____ and _____

(2) It was cold, so we sat in front of the fireplace to get warm.

_____ and _____

(3) We ran uphill, and at the top we rested.

_____ and _____

(4) My teacher said I needed a notebook.

_____ and _____

(5) We are at the beach and I want to make a sandcastle.

_____ and _____

2 Read the paragraph below. Then write the compound words.

10 points for completion

> It was my birthday. We ran uphill to the playground to have some fun. I had some blueberry ice cream. Then we played some football. We even saw a rainbow!

birthday _____ _____

_____ _____ _____

3 Combine the words from the box to make compound words. Write them in the space below.

45 points for completion

snow	moon	base	shoe	grand
sun	ball	flake	mother	bulb
father	light			

_____   _____   _____

_____   _____   _____

_____   _____   _____

4 Complete each sentence using a word from the box.

5 points per question

downstairs	notebook	birthday
bluebird	snowball	

(1) Mom gave me a new _____ for school.

(2) Steve made a _____ out of snow.

(3) I am happy. It is my _____ today!

(4) The kitchen is _____.

(5) A _____ landed on Emily's window.

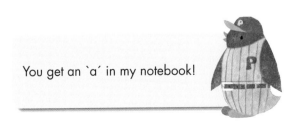

You get an `a´ in my notebook!

27

14 Synonyms

Level ★★

Date / /

Name

Score /100

1 Read the sentences. In each sentence, trace the word that means the **same** as the one underlined.

3 points per question

(1) I like <u>cold</u> water best. It tastes good when it is ___icy___!

(2) That horse is <u>big</u>. How did it get so ___large___?

(3) Is that log <u>strong</u>? I hope it is ___sturdy___.

(4) That baby has such <u>pink</u> cheeks.

Her ___rosy___ cheeks are so cute.

(5) I just want a <u>little</u> taste.

Will you give me a ___small___ bite?

2 Draw a line between the two words that mean the **same**.

5 points per question

(1) big   •

(2) skinny •

(3) pick •

(4) talk •

(5) chilly •

(6) glad •

(7) loud •

•ⓐ thin

•ⓑ large

•ⓒ speak

•ⓓ cool

•ⓔ noisy

•ⓕ happy

•ⓖ choose

3 Read the sentences. Write the word from the box that means the **same** as the one underlined.

5 points per question

close	house	lift	pull
road	seat	shake	

(1) <u>Drag</u> the rug, and then _____ the rope.

(2) <u>Raise</u> the flag, and then _____ the box.

(3) The baby likes to _____ and <u>rattle</u> the toy.

(4) I want to go <u>home</u> to my _____.

(5) Do you want to sit in this _____ or that <u>chair</u>?

(6) Green <u>Street</u> is a wide _____.

(7) Please _____ the door. I want it <u>shut</u>.

4 Read all the phrases. Draw a line to match the phrases that mean the **same**. Then read the phrases aloud.

5 points per question

(1) one small mouse
and another tiny mouse
    •ⓐ lots of baby cats

(2) many kittens •
    •ⓑ two little mice

(3) a goose, a parrot
and a duck
    •ⓒ three birds

You are quick!

1 Draw a line between the two words that mean the **opposite**.

2 points per question

(1) up • •ⓐ bottom   (2) over • •ⓑ slow
(3) left • •ⓒ down   (4) smile • •ⓓ under
(5) happy• •ⓔ right   (6) hot • •ⓕ quiet
(7) in • •ⓖ unhappy   (8) loud • •ⓗ cold
(9) top • •ⓘ out   (10) fast • •ⓙ frown

2 What is going on in the park? Write each word from the picture in the correct sentence below.

5 points per question

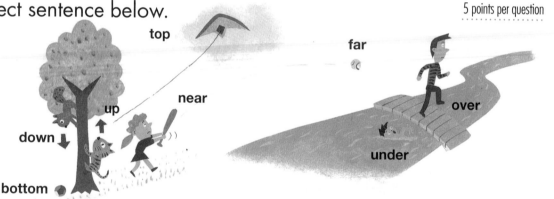

(1) The cat climbs _____ the tree.

(2) The squirrel climbs _____ the tree.

(3) The tall man walks _____ the bridge.

(4) The short boy swims _____ the bridge.

(5) The kite is flying near the _____ of the tree.

(6) The ball is at the _____ of the tree.

(7) The girl is _____. The girl hit the ball _____.

3 Draw a line from the phrase on the left to the phrase on the right that means the **opposite**. Use the pictures as clues.

3 points per question

(1) hot soup •   • ⓐ over the branch

(2) under the branch •   • ⓑ the back of the chair

(3) inside the car •   • ⓒ cold soup

(4) the front of the chair •   • ⓓ outside the car

(5) run upstairs •   • ⓔ run downstairs

4 Complete the sentences using the words in the box. Use the word in the box that means the **opposite** of the underlined word.

5 points per question

downstairs	slow	loud	unhappy	left	outside

(1) The toy goes <u>inside</u> the box, not _____.

(2) Put the fork on the _____ and the spoon on the <u>right</u>.

(3) One girl is <u>happy</u>. One girl is _____.

(4) The mouse is <u>quiet</u>. The lion is _____.

(5) The snail is _____. The kitten is <u>quick</u>.

(6) Jill runs <u>upstairs</u>.
Jack runs _____.

You figured it out!

1 Read each sentence. Trace the word that means the **same** as the underlined word.

5 points per question

(1) The <u>noisy</u> man is __loud__.

(2) The <u>small</u> mouse is __little__.

(3) The <u>icy</u> drink is __cold__.

(4) The <u>happy</u> girl is __joyful__.

(5) The <u>unhappy</u> man is __sad__.

(6) The <u>damp</u> dog is __wet__.

2 Read the sentences. If both underlined words mean the **same**, circle the "**S**." If the words are **opposites**, circle the "**O**."

6 points per question

(1) My bedroom is <u>upstairs</u>. The bathroom is <u>downstairs</u>.   **S**   **O**

(2) My house is <u>near</u>, but the school is <u>far</u>.   **S**   **O**

(3) I feel <u>chilly</u>. It is <u>cool</u> out here.   **S**   **O**

(4) I like to <u>yell</u> and <u>shout</u>!   **S**   **O**

(5) The <u>wet</u> dog got <u>dry</u> in the sun.   **S**   **O**

3 Read each sentence. Then fill in the opposite word using a word from the sentence above. 5 points per question

(1) Our cat sleeps in the daytime but plays in the nighttime.

The **opposite** of daytime is nighttime.

(2) Even when I am wide awake, my brother can still be fast asleep.

The **opposite** of awake is _____.

(3) There are many toys in her room, but few of them work.

The **opposite** of many is _____.

(4) The bus is always full, but today it is empty.

The **opposite** of full is _____.

(5) Jack always trips on the same log, but Jill never does.

The **opposite** of always is _____.

(6) Put the tiny, black rock on that huge gray stone.

The **opposite** of tiny is _____.

4 Color all the word pairs that are the **same** yellow. Color all the word pairs that are **opposites** blue. What do you see? 10 points for completion

Not bad at all!

_____

1 In the second sentence, write the word that means the **opposite** of the underlined word in the first sentence.

6 points per question

| scary | heavy | finish | away | hard |

(1) The boys went <u>toward</u> the food.
They went _____ from the girls.

(2) Jen can <u>start</u> eating her food.
She can never _____ her food.

(3) Dogs are very <u>friendly</u> and like to lick your hand.
Dogs can also be _____ sometimes.

(4) This homework is not <u>easy</u>. It is _____.

(5) This box is not <u>light</u>. It is very _____.

2 Read the sentences. If both underlined words mean the **same**, circle the "**S**." If the words are **opposites**, circle the "**O**."

6 points per question

(1) My glass is <u>full</u> and my plate is <u>empty</u>.　　**S**　　**O**

(2) My sister <u>always</u> brushes her teeth.
My little brother <u>never</u> does.　　**S**　　**O**

(3) Dad has to <u>go</u> to work. He will <u>return</u> soon.　　**S**　　**O**

(4) Most kids think cats are <u>friendly</u>.
I think they are <u>scary</u>.　　**S**　　**O**

(5) Did you stay to the <u>finish</u> of the game?
I stayed all the way until the <u>end</u>.　　**S**　　**O**

3 Match the sentences below that mean the **opposite**. 4 points per question

(1) I went outside. •   • ⓐ I always brush my teeth.

(2) I am scary. •   • ⓑ I am returning from school.

(3) My backpack is heavy. •   • ⓒ I went inside.

(4) I am going to school. •   • ⓓ My backpack is light.

(5) I never brush my teeth. •   • ⓔ I am friendly.

4 Complete each sentence using a word from the box. 4 points per question

friendly	full	most	never	huge

(1) Mr. Jones has a _____ truck. It is very big.

(2) I ate too much! I am so _____.

(3) Our dog is _____. He licks everyone.

(4) I did _____ of my work. Do I still get ice cream?

(5) Mrs. Donna told me _____ to hit anyone.

Wow, that's huge!

35

18 Irregular Plurals

Level ☆☆

Date / /

Name

Score /100

1 Complete the chart below. See how the word **bush** changes when there is more than one.

2 points per question

One	More than one
bush	(1) bushes
bench	(2) benches
dish	(3) dishes
tomato	(4) tomatoes

One	More than one
baby	(5) babies
story	(6) stories
candy	(7) candies
bunny	(8) bunnies

2 Complete each sentence using a word from the box.

6 points per question

churches dishes cities candies potatoes ladies

(1) We all washed the ____________ after lunch.

(2) Farmer John likes his little town.
The __________ are too big!

(3) Allison likes to visit different _______________ on Sundays.

(4) French fries are good, but I don't like ______________.

(5) The __________ looked very nice in their dresses.

(6) I like chewy _______________ the best.

3 Complete the chart below.

3 points per question

One	More than one		One	More than one
wish	(1)		(5)	babies
(2)	benches		story	(6)
match	(3)		(7)	candies
(4)	potatoes		family	(8)

4 Pick the correct word to complete each sentence below.

3 points per question

(1) What time is it? I don't have a _____.
[watch / watches]

(2) Mrs. Davis has a new _____!
[baby / babies]

(3) There are three _____ in front of the library.
[bench / benches]

(4) I always get to hear two _____ before bed.
[story / stories]

(5) How many _____ should we put in the salad?
[tomato / tomatoes]

(6) Jane wants a big _____ for her birthday.
[party / parties]

(7) You have so many _____ for your hair!
[brush / brushes]

(8) It is very sunny at the _____.
[beach / beaches]

Well done!

37

19

Who / When / Where
Baseball 1

Level ☆☆

Date　　/　　/

Name

Score

/100

1 Read the passage. Then answer the questions using words from the passage.

10 points per question

> Games like baseball have been played for a long time. Some think the first baseball game was played by two teams from New York. Many of the rules of this sport were made a long time ago.

(1) Where did the first baseball teams come from?

The first baseball teams came from _____.

(2) When were many of the rules of baseball made?

Many of the rules were made a long _____.

2 For each word below, choose a word in bold from the passage that has a similar meaning.

10 points per question

> A pitcher pitches, or **throws**, the ball to the batter on the other team. The batter hits, or **bats**, the ball into the field. Then the batter tries to run past all four bases. Both teams try to get, or **score**, as many runs as they can.

(1) pitches　　_____

(2) hits　　_____

(3) get　　_____

3 Read the passage below. Then answer the questions using words from the passage.

15 points per question

If the batter swings the bat but misses the ball, it is a "strike." Once the batter has three strikes, the team gets an out. Then another batter tries to hit the ball. After three outs, the teams change sides.

The pitcher tries to throw the ball so that the batter cannot hit it. The ball may twist or spin from side to side. A fastball can move as fast as a train.

(1) When does the team get an "out"?
The team gets an "out" once the batter has _____.

(2) When do the teams change sides?
Teams change sides after _____.

4 Read the passage below. Then answer the questions using words from the passage.

10 points per question

After the ball is hit, the batter tries to run past all the bases. If the ball is hit out of the field, the batter gets a home run. Babe Ruth was known for his home runs. Each year, he hit more and more home runs. In his best year, he hit 60 home runs in 154 games. No one could do any better for a long time.

(1) Where must a batter hit a ball to get a home run?
A batter must hit a ball _____ of the field to get home run.

(2) How many home runs did Babe Ruth hit in his best year?
In his best year, he hit _____ home runs.

Your team won the game!

Who / When / Where
Baseball 2

20

Level ☆☆

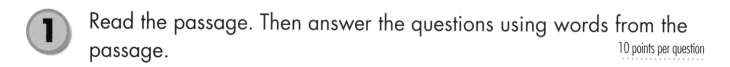

Date / /

Name

Score /100

1 Read the passage. Then answer the questions using words from the passage.

10 points per question

> There are many songs about the game of baseball. A long time ago, Jack Norworth wrote the song "Take Me Out to the Ball Game." He was riding on a train in New York when he made it up. He wrote over 2,500 songs, but this one was the best known.

（1） What is the song "Take Me Out to the Ball Game" about?

The song is about the game of _____.

（2） When did Jack Norworth write the song?

He wrote it while he was riding on _____ in New York.

2 Write the underlined words in the blanks in the song below.

10 points per question

 crowd = a large group

 team = a group of players on one side

 game = a contest between two teams

> "Take Me Out to the Ball Game"
> Take me out to the ball game,
> Take me out with the （1） _____.
> Buy me some peanuts and cracker jacks,
> I don't care if I never get back,
> Let me root, root, root for the home （2） _____,
> If they don't win it's a shame.
> For it's one, two, three strikes, you're out,
> At the old ball （3） _____.

3 Read the passage below. Then answer the questions using words from the passage.

10 points per question

"Take Me Out to the Ball Game"
Take me out to the ball game,
Take me out with the crowd.
Buy me some peanuts and cracker jacks,
I don't care if I never get back,
Let me root, root, root for the home team,
If they don't win it's a shame.
For it's one, two, three strikes, you're out,
At the old ball game.

PEANUTS

(1) Where does the singer want to go?
The singer wants to go to the _____.

(2) How many strikes until you are out?
It is _____ strikes and you are out.

(3) They sell hot dogs or popcorn or other snacks at games. In the song, what are some of the snacks sold at ball games?
Some of the snacks sold at ball games are _____
and _____ jacks.

4 Complete each sentence using a word from the box.

5 points per question

| baseball | strikes | popcorn | peanuts |

(1) A salty snack made from corn is called _____.

(2) The game of _____ uses a bat and a ball.

(3) My favorite nuts are _____.

(4) It's three _____ and you are out.

Do you like baseball? I do!

41

What / Why
All Kinds of Storms

21

Level

Score

/ 100

Date / /

Name

1 Read the passage. Then complete the statements using words from the passage.

8 points per question

There are many kinds of storms. Some storms can happen at any time. Windstorms may have strong winds, but no rain. A "Winter Storm Watch" means there is a chance of heavy snow or ice. When the snow piles up slowly, there is time to get to a safe place. In a heavy snowstorm, the snow can pile up quickly. There may not be time to get to a safe place. Wind can blow the snow into huge piles called snowdrifts. Snowdrifts can block doors. In a bad snowstorm, it is best to stay inside.

(1) In a _____, strong winds blow, but there may be no rain.

(2) During a "Winter Storm Watch," there may be heavy _____ or _____.

(3) Lots of snow can fall in a _____.

(4) In a heavy snowstorm, there may not be time to get to a _____.

(5) A _____ is a huge pile of snow that can block a door.

2 Read the passage. Then answer the questions using words from the passage.

12 points per question

When it rains for a long time, rivers and streams can fill up. There may be more water than the ground can hold. Water can spill out of the stream and into the street. A little pool of water is called a puddle. A whole new stream or lake is called a flood. Floods may be just a few inches deep or as high as a house. Water from floods can be fast and strong. It can wash out a bridge or carry a bus down the street.

When there is a big storm, it is a good idea to stay home. Find a flashlight in case the lights go out. You can also store clean water to drink.

(1) What is a puddle?
A puddle is a little _____ on the ground.

(2) What can happen to rivers and streams when it rains for a long time?
When it rains for a long time, rivers and streams can _____.
Then water can _____ out of the stream and into the street.

(3) How deep are floods?
Floods can be just a _____ deep or as _____ as a house.

(4) Why is it good to have a flashlight?
It is good to have a flashlight in case the _____.

(5) What can you store to drink?
You can store _____ to drink.

Storms can be scary!

What / Why
A Day at the Beach

22

Date / /

Name

Level ☆ ☆

Score /100

1 Read the passage. Then answer the questions using words from the passage.

10 points per question

> Peter is very happy. Today his family is going to the beach! They pack swim trunks, towels and hats. They pack some balls and some card games. They pack food and lots of water. They pack an umbrella so that they will have shade. Peter even brings his pet rock, Charlie. It is a sunny and hot day, just right for the beach. They get in the car and drive all morning.
>
> When they get to the beach, Peter puts all of his things on the towel. He takes his pail and shovel out. Then he walks to the edge of the water to build a sandcastle.

(1) What kind of games does the family bring to the beach?
The family brings some _____ and some _____ games.

(2) What pet does Peter bring to the beach?
Peter brings his _____, Charlie, to the beach.

(3) What does the family bring so that they will have shade?
The family brings an _____.

(4) What kind of day is perfect for the beach?
A _____ and _____ day is perfect for the beach.

(5) Where does Peter walk once he puts his things on the towel?
Peter walks to the _____ of the water to build
a _____.

2 Read the passage. Then answer the questions using words from the passage.

10 points per question

First, Peter builds a sandcastle. It is very big and has three towers. Then the water comes too close and his castle falls down.

"That's okay," says Peter, "it's time to get in the water!" He jumps into the water and splashes his dad. They swim in the water for a while. Then it is time for lunch. They eat some apples, pears and grapes. The food tastes good, and it makes Peter tired. He takes a little nap on the towel.

When he wakes up, it is time to leave. He starts to pack up, but where is Charlie? Oh no! They look and look, but his mom says they have to leave. He is sad, but Charlie is not sure where he left him. He can find a new pet rock at home.

They finish packing. Then his mom picks up the towel to go. There is Charlie, sitting under the towel!

(1) Why does Peter's castle fall down?
Peter's castle falls down because the _____ comes too _____.

(2) What does Peter do after he builds his castle?
Peter _____ into the water and _____ his dad.

(3) What does Peter's family eat for lunch?
Peter's family eats some _____, pears and _____.

(4) What can Peter find at home?
Peter can find a _____ at home.

(5) Where is Charlie found?
Charlie is found sitting under the _____.

What do you like to do at the beach?

_____

Who / What / When / Where / Why
Two Frogs

23

Level ☆☆

Score

Date / /

Name

/100

1 Read the passage. Then answer the questions using words from the passage.

10 points per question

> Once upon a time, there were two frogs.
>
> One frog lived in Tampa by the beach. The other lived in a pond in Winter Park. The frogs had never met each other. They decided to go and see other places.
>
> The Tampa frog wanted to see Winter Park. The Winter Park frog wanted to see Tampa. Both frogs set out on the road that linked their two cities.
>
> The two frogs met on the top of a hill. They stopped to talk. The Tampa frog said that he was on his way to see Winter Park. The Winter Park frog said that he was on his way to see Tampa.

(1) When did this story happen?

This story happened _____ a time.

(2) Where did the Tampa frog live?

The Tampa frog lived in Tampa by the _____.

(3) Why did the two frogs leave their homes?

They decided to go and see _____.

(4) Who met on the top of a hill?

The _____ met on the top of a hill.

(5) What did the two frogs do on the top of the hill?

The two frogs _____ to talk on the top of the hill.

2 Read the passage. Then answer the questions using words from the passage.

10 points per question

"It is too bad that we are not taller," said the Tampa frog. "We might be able to see both cities from here if we were."

"We can fix that," said the frog from Winter Park. "We can stand up on our back legs to look."

The Tampa frog faced Winter Park, and the Winter Park frog faced Tampa. They held each other up and looked at the cities down the road. The silly thing is that they did not think about the fact that their eyes were on the tops of their heads! Each frog was looking back at his own city.

"Oh dear," said the Tampa frog, "Winter Park looks the same as Tampa. I don't want to go there."

The Winter Park frog said, "Tampa is just the same as Winter Park. I don't want to go there."

The frogs did not want to go to a city that looked the same as their own. They both returned home.

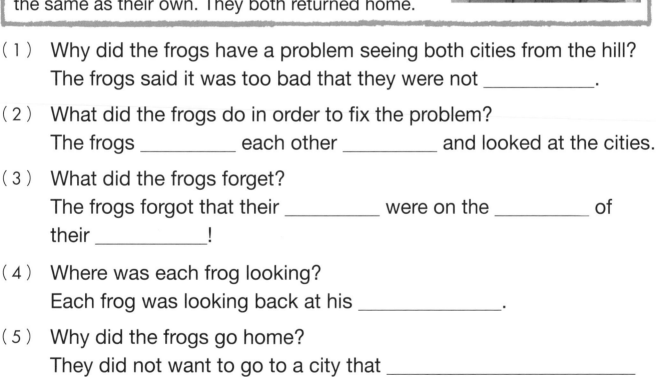

(1) Why did the frogs have a problem seeing both cities from the hill?
The frogs said it was too bad that they were not _____.

(2) What did the frogs do in order to fix the problem?
The frogs _____ each other _____ and looked at the cities.

(3) What did the frogs forget?
The frogs forgot that their _____ were on the _____ of their _____!

(4) Where was each frog looking?
Each frog was looking back at his _____.

(5) Why did the frogs go home?
They did not want to go to a city that _____ as their own city.

How far do you want to go?

_____

Who / What / When / Where / Why
Bees!

24

Level ★★★

Score

Date / /

Name

/100

1 Read the passage. Then answer the questions using words from the passage.

10 points per question

Bees are very important little animals.

They can be scary, too. They buzz and they also sting.

When they sting, it can hurt, but we need bees.

Why do we need bees? We need bees because they help spread flowers.

Flowers have pollen in them. Pollen is needed to make a new flower. If you spread pollen, you help new flowers grow. Bees get pollen on them when they search for food. When they land on another flower, they put pollen on that flower.

In this way, bees help flowers grow!

Did you know that bees were so important?

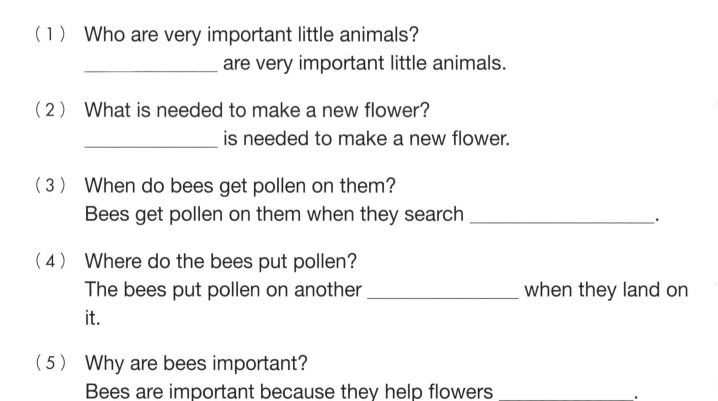

(1) Who are very important little animals?

_____ are very important little animals.

(2) What is needed to make a new flower?

_____ is needed to make a new flower.

(3) When do bees get pollen on them?

Bees get pollen on them when they search _____.

(4) Where do the bees put pollen?

The bees put pollen on another _____ when they land on it.

(5) Why are bees important?

Bees are important because they help flowers _____.

2 Read the passage. Then answer the questions using words from the passage.

10 points per question

Trent wants to be just like his uncle. His uncle Stan is an artist. He draws comic book art. His best comic book told the story of a man who was bitten by a dog and got super powers.

Trent draws a little bit every day after school. "Draw every day," his uncle always says. So every day, Trent uses his pencils and his paint. The walls in his room are full of comics. Some of them are his. Some are his uncle's. Some are there to remind Trent to work hard.

What will his first comic book be about? Trent is not sure. He might draw a book about a young man who wants to be a comic book artist. In his story, the man is working hard when a bee flies in the window. The bee stings him on the hand and gives him powers. Trent is just not sure that "Bee Man" is a good title.

(1) Who does Trent want to be like?
Trent wants to be like his _____.

(2) What does his uncle do?
Trent's uncle draws _____ art.

(3) Where does Trent put his drawings?
Trent puts his drawings on the _____ in his _____.

(4) When does Trent draw?
Trent draws every day _____.

(5) Why is Trent not sure about his new comic book?
Trent is not sure that "Bee Man" is a _____.

What do you want to be?

_____

1 Read the following Table of Contents. Then answer the questions below.

10 points per question

Frog and Flea and the Hole

• • • • •

Chapter	Page
Frog and Flea Go on a Walk	2
Frog Falls Asleep	10
Flea Falls in a Hole	14
Frog Looks for Flea	19
No Rope in Sight	24
Frog Finds Five Friends	28
Together They Get Flea Out	32
Home at Last	38

(1) What is the title, or the name, of this book?
The title of this book is "Frog and _____ and the _____."

(2) What page does the story start on?
The story starts on page _____.

(3) What is the name of the first chapter?
The first chapter is named " _____ and Flea Go on a _____."

(4) What page does the chapter called "No Rope in Sight" start on?
"No Rope in Sight" starts on page _____.

(5) Based on this table of contents, do you think Frog helps Flea get out of the hole?
_____.

2 Read the following hints. Then fill in the missing information on the Table of Contents below.

10 points per question

ⓐ The first chapter is called "Sunny Day."

ⓑ The second chapter starts on page 5.

ⓒ The chapter called "Flea Takes Over" starts 6 pages after the chapter called "Frog Flies a Kite."

ⓓ "The Kite is Stuck" is the name of the chapter after the chapter called "Where is the Kite?".

ⓔ The last chapter starts on page 32.

Frog and Flea and the Flying Fox

• • • • •

Chapter	Page
(1) _____	2
Frog and Flea Climb a Tree	(2) ____
Frog Flies a Kite	10
Flea Takes Over	(3) ____
Where is the Kite?	19
(4) _____	23
Frog Finds a Fox	28
Together They Figure it Out	(5) ____

Now you can tell what is in a book!

Sequence
The Lemonade Stand / Time for School!

26

Level ★★★

Date / /

Name

Score / 100

1 Read the passage and take a look at the pictures. Then number the pictures below in the order in which they happened.

60 points for completion

The Lemonade Stand

Henry wanted a new baseball glove. He asked his friend Dave to help him run a lemonade stand. Together they took a table and some chairs outside. Then they painted a sign. They made sweet lemonade, and everyone wanted some. In the end, Henry got his glove!

(1)   (1)

(2)   ( )

(3)   ( )

(4)   ( )

(5)   ( )

(6)   ( )

2 Read the passage. Then number the pictures below in the order in which they happened in the passage.

40 points for completion

Time for School!

Kevin jumped out of bed. It was Friday and it was time to get ready for school. He went to the bathroom, where his mom was waiting for him with his toothbrush.

"You will brush for two minutes, right?" she asked him.

"Yes," he groaned. He hated brushing his teeth.

He washed his face and ran back to his room. His mom had put out his best shirt and a nice pair of pants. He liked the shirt with the football on it best.

After he got dressed, he went down the stairs two at a time. His mom made pancakes for him! With berries! He was eating so many pancakes he almost forgot about the bus. He jumped up and ran out the door. His backpack! He ran back inside and his mom was smiling and waiting with his backpack.

Kevin was lucky today. When he ran back outside, the bus was there.

(1) ( )   (2) ( )   (3) ( )   (4) ( )

(5) ( )   (6) ( )   (7) ( )   (8) ( )

53

Reading Comprehension
The Ant and the Grasshopper

27

Level ☆☆☆

Date / /

Name

Score /100

1 Read the passage. Then answer the questions using words from the passage.

8 points per question

> One summer day, a grasshopper was hopping about, chirping and singing and having fun. An ant passed by. He was taking some corn to his nest. The ant was tired, but he kept working and kept walking with the corn to his home.
>
> "Why not come and play and sing with me?" asked the grasshopper. "You don't have to work so hard in the summer." "It is not time for work, silly ant. It is time for play!" added the grasshopper.
>
> "I am helping to store food for the winter," said the ant, "and I think you should help us."
>
> The grasshopper went back to singing and resting in the field.

(1) Where was the ant taking his corn?
He was taking it to his _____.

(2) What was the grasshopper doing?
He was chirping, _____, and having fun.

(3) What did the grasshopper think the ant should not do in the summer?
He said the ant should not _____ so hard.

(4) Why was the ant working so hard?
He was helping to store food for the _____.

(5) Did the grasshopper help the ant?
_____. The grasshopper went back to singing and _____ in the field.

2 Read the passage. Then answer the questions using words from the passage.

12 points per question

> "Why bother about winter?" said the grasshopper. "Don't worry. We have plenty of food right now," he added.
>
> But the ant went on its way and continued to work. When the winter came, the grasshopper had no food. He was very hungry, and he came back to find the ant. He found the ant happy and eating corn and grain. "Can I have some corn?" asked the grasshopper. "I am sorry grasshopper, but you did not help me in the summer when I worked very hard. You sat and sang when I asked you to help. I stored this food all summer. Now I will eat it when there is no more food to find," said the ant.
>
> That's when the grasshopper understood.
>
> It is good to save for times when there will be no food.

(1) Why did the grasshopper think he did not need to worry?
The grasshopper did not think he needed to worry because he had
_____ of _____ in the summer.

(2) When did the grasshopper come back to find the ant?
The grasshopper came back in the _____ to find the ant.

(3) How did the ant have food when there was no food to find?
The ant had food because he _____ food all summer.

(4) Why didn't the ant give the grasshopper some food?
The ant did not give the grasshopper food because the grasshopper
did not _____ him in the summer when he _____ very hard.

(5) What did the grasshopper understand?
The grasshopper finally understood that it is _____ to _____
for times when there will be no food.

Good job reading!

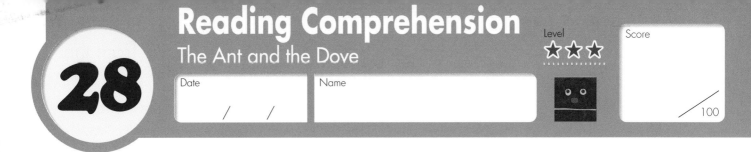

Reading Comprehension
The Ant and the Dove

Level ☆☆☆

Score
/100

Date   /   /

Name

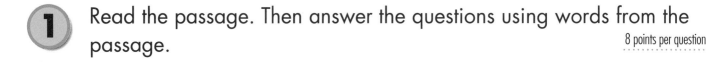

1 Read the passage. Then answer the questions using words from the passage.

8 points per question

> One day, a red ant was walking along the river. He was thinking about how he wished he had more friends. Rivers can be scary when you are a small ant, but the ant was not looking where he was walking. He slipped and fell into the river!
>
> He was very scared because he could not swim very well. The ant tried his best, but he could not get back to the bank of the river.
>
> A dove was flying over the river and saw the ant. He wanted to help. The bird found a leaf and dropped it into the river to help the ant.
>
> The ant got out of the water and onto the leaf.
>
> He thanked the bird again and again.
>
> "You saved my life! Thank you very much," he said.

(1) What was the ant thinking about as he was walking?

He was thinking about how he wanted to have _____.

(2) Why did the ant fall into the river?

He was not _____ where he was _____.

(3) Why was the ant scared?

He was scared because he could not _____.

(4) Who was flying over the river?

A _____ was flying over the river.

(5) How did the dove save the ant?

The dove dropped a _____ into the _____ for the ant.

2 Read the passage. Then answer the questions using words from the passage.

12 points per question

A little bit later, the ant and his leaf finally made it to the bank of the river. At the side of the river, the ant got out and rested. He was very tired from all the fuss. He saw a strange man with a net in his hands. The man was looking up at the dove. The man started to set the net up in a tree and the dove did not see him. "What is that man trying to do?" wondered the ant. When the man started calling to the dove, the ant understood. He was trying to catch the dove!

The ant wasted no time. He ran over to the man and sunk his teeth into the man's leg. The man was very angry and dropped the net. He hopped around on one foot, and the dove saw him.

"Thank you for saving me. You are a good friend!" called the dove. The ant was happy.

(1) Why was the ant tired?

The ant was tired from all of the _____.

(2) What did the man have in his hands?

The man had a _____ in his _____.

(3) Why did the man have a net in his hands?

The man was _____ to _____ the dove!

(4) What did the ant do to save the dove?

The ant _____ his _____ into the man's leg.

(5) Why was the ant happy in the end?

The dove said he was a _____.

Good job!

Reading Comprehension
Every Dog Should Have a Child 1

29

Level ☆☆☆

Date / /

Name

Score /100

1 Read the passage. Then answer the questions using words from the passage.

8 points per question

> Some people say that every child needs a dog. Well, I say that every dog needs a child. I am a dog and this is my child! We are best friends.
>
> The best child is nice and can learn quickly. I feel that a child must like to share his or her snacks with me. I try to teach my child to give me snacks. Often, she does. I got the pick of the litter!
>
> My child is kind and shares her ice cream with me. I love strawberry ice cream. She is learning to enjoy eating it, too.

(1) Who is telling the story?

A _____ is telling the story.

(2) What does every dog need?

Every dog needs a _____.

(3) What makes the best child?

The best child is _____ and can _____ quickly.

(4) What does the dog try to teach his child?

The dog tries to teach his child to give him _____.

(5) Why does the dog say his child is kind?

The dog says his child is kind because she _____ her ice cream with him.

Read the passage. Then answer the questions using words from the passage.

12 points per question

> I can teach my child many tricks just by putting my chin on her lap! I am teaching my child to play fetch. She stands in the backyard and throws the stick. She is learning to say "bring" every time I pick up the stick. My child is a quick learner!
>
> We never play fetch just once. We always play it over and over. Sometimes she doesn't throw the stick very well, so I don't bring it right back to her. Soon she gets it right. But she tires out before I do. I guess a child is just not as strong as a dog!

(1)   What does the dog do to teach the child tricks?
The dog puts his _____ on the child's lap.

(2)   Does the child throw the stick or pick it up?
The child _____.

(3)   When does the child say "bring"?
The child says "_____" when the dog picks up the _____.

(4)   Do the dog and child play fetch just once, or do they play it over and over?
They play it _____.

(5)   When doesn't the dog bring the stick right back to the child?
The dog doesn't bring the stick right back when the child _____ the stick very well.

That was just right!

Reading Comprehension
Every Dog Should Have a Child 2

30

Level
★★☆

Score

/100

Date   /   /

Name

1 Read the passage. Then answer the questions using words from the passage.

8 points per question

> When I take my child out for a walk, we need to stay close together. That is why I use a leash and collar. My collar connects me to my child. She loops the other end of the leash around her hand. Now I know she won't run off without me.
>
> Sometimes my child tugs at my leash. She has a hard time keeping up with me. I cannot run too fast for her, or she will get hurt. I am quickly learning the art of "walking the child."

(1) When does the dog need to stay close to the child?
They need to stay close when they go out for a _____.

(2) What does the dog use to stay close to his child?
The dog uses a _____ and _____.

(3) Where does the child loop the other end of the leash?
The child loops it around _____.

(4) When does the child tug at the leash?
She tugs at the leash when she has a _____ keeping up with the dog.

(5) Why can't the dog run too fast?
The dog can't run too fast or the child _____.

2 Read the passage. Then answer the questions using words from the passage.

12 points per question

Some days, my child runs too fast in front of me. I don't think it is safe to run so fast near a street, so I stop suddenly! When she falls down on the sidewalk, I lick her face to help her feel better. Then we go home right away!

It is not easy to teach a child, but I am a very lucky dog. Even though I have to tell her many things over and over, a soft bark is all she needs to let her know what to do!

(1) Does the child go too fast or too slow?
The child runs _____.

(2) Does the child stand on the street or fall down the sidewalk?
The child _____ on the sidewalk.

(3) Does the dog help the child feel better or worse?
The dog helps the child _____.

(4) In this story, who teaches whom?
In this story, _____ teaches the _____.

(5) Why is the dog lucky?
The dog is lucky because a _____ is all the child needs to learn what to do.

You learn quickly!

Reading Comprehension
Stone Soup 1

Level

☆☆☆

Score

/100

31

Date / /

Name

1 Read the passage. Then complete the sentences below with words from the passage.

12 points per question

> Once there was a poor town. There wasn't enough food to eat. People hid what little they had.
> No one shared.
>
> One day, a strange young man came to the town. No one said, "Hello." "Was he a robber?" they asked. "Did he want to take their food?" When the man waved, they all yelled, "Go away! We have no food!"
>
> "That's okay," said the stranger. "I can make stone soup."
>
> "What is stone soup?" one woman asked.

(1) Was the town rich or poor?
The town was _____.

(2) Did people share their food or hide it?
People _____ what little food they had.

(3) A young man _____ to the town. People yelled,
"Go _____!"

(4) People wondered if the man was a _____, or if he wanted
to _____ their food.

(5) Did the man steal things or wave?
He _____.

2 Read the passage. Then number the pictures in the order in which they happened in the passage.

40 points for completion

"This is stone soup," he said. Then he took a big pot from his backpack. He found firewood and made a fire. He poured water in the pot. Then he looked for a large, white stone. He put the stone in the pot. As the water boiled, he sat back and smiled.

"I like my stone soup," he said. "I have made it for kings and queens. I can almost smell it. Now if I just had a little salt…"

"If I give you my salt, may I share your soup?" asked one woman.

"Of course!" he said. The woman put a tiny pinch of salt into the pot.

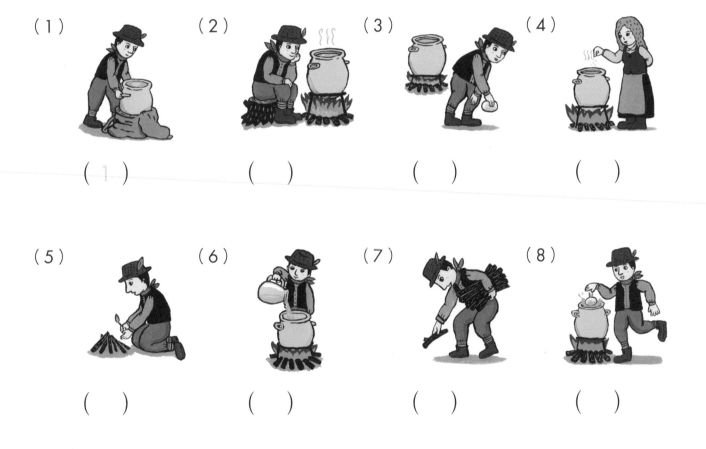

(1)　　(1)

(2)　　( )

(3)　　( )

(4)　　( )

(5)　　( )

(6)　　( )

(7)　　( )

(8)　　( )

I am hungry!

Reading Comprehension
Stone Soup 2

32

Level ☆☆☆

Date / /

Name

Score /100

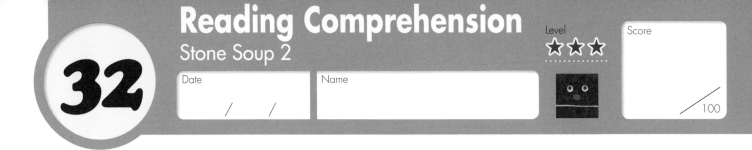

1 Read the passage. Then answer the questions using words from the passage.

10 points per question

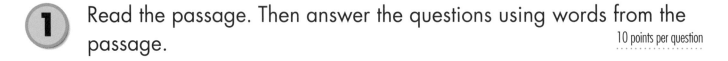

A little girl smelled the soup and then ran home.

"I found some yummy carrots," she said when she came back. Then she sat down next to the woman to sniff the smell of the soup.

One by one, the men and women in the town all found a scrap of food to share. They gave the man three dry peas and a little rice. They gave him a red pepper and a green pepper and a yellow pepper. They gave him an old beef bone and butter. Soon the pot boiled full of good things to eat.

(1) Did the girl run home to get the carrots or sit and wait for them?
   The little girl _____.

(2) Did the people hide their scraps or share them?
   The people in the town all found a scrap of food to _____.

(3) Was there a lot of rice or a little?
   There was a _____ rice.

(4) Was the beef bone old or new?
   The beef bone was _____.

(5) Was the pot empty or full?
   The pot _____ of good things to eat.

2 Read the passage. Then complete the sentences below using words from the passage.

10 points per question

"There is enough soup for all," said the young man. "Please join me."

They all set up tables with their best dishes and spoons.

"This is the best stone soup we have ever tasted," they cried. "How can such poor people be as lucky as kings to eat such good food?"

The soup was made with salt and pepper, peas and rice, and carrots and beans. It was made with butter and oil, peppers, an old beef bone, and last but not least, a stone. When the young man had to go, he left the stone with the little girl and her family.

(1) How much soup did the man make?
He made _____ soup _____.

(2) The people set up tables with their best _____ and spoons.

(3) The town's people asked how such _____ people could eat such _____.

(4) What was the most important part of the soup?
Last but not least, the soup was made with _____.

(5) When the young man had to go, where did he leave the stone?
When the young man had to go, he left the stone with the _____ and her _____.

Time for soup!

Reading Comprehension
The Velveteen Rabbit 1

33

Level ★ ★ ★

Date   /   /

Name

Score   /100

1 Read the passage. Then answer the questions using words from the passage.

8 points per question

> When Matt turned four, his grandmother gave him a stuffed rabbit for his birthday. The rabbit was so soft! His fur had brown and white spots. His ears were lined with smooth pink silk. For a whole hour, Matt loved him. Then the rabbit was put on a high shelf in the boy's bedroom.
>
> The rabbit was shy, and new to the room. He waited for the other toys to greet him, but they didn't. The other toys were mean. The only toy that was nice to him was an old skin horse. The skin horse was the oldest toy in the room. It was a gift from Matt's father. The father had played with the horse when he was a boy. The skin horse's coat was worn thin. He was old and wise. He had seen many shiny, cheap new toys come in, brag loudly, and then break or rust. He knew how toys were made real.

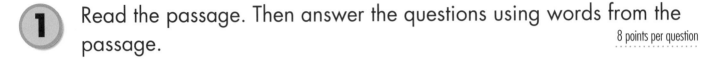

(1) When did Matt get the stuffed rabbit?

Matt got the stuffed rabbit for his fourth _____.

(2) For how long did Matt love the rabbit that day?

Matt loved him for a _____.

(3) Where was the rabbit put?

The rabbit was put on a _____.

(4) Who gave Matt the skin horse?

Matt's _____ gave Matt the skin horse.

(5) Who knew how toys were made real?

The old skin _____ knew how toys were made real.

2 Read the passage. Then answer the questions using words from the passage.

12 points per question

"What is 'Real?'" asked the rabbit one day. "Does it mean having things that buzz and move inside?"

"'Real' isn't how you are made," said the horse. "It is what happens to you. When a child loves you for a long, long time, not just to play with, then you become Real."

"Does it happen all at once? Or bit by bit?" asked the rabbit.

"It happens bit by bit and takes a long time. It can take months or years. It does not happen to toys that break easily. By the time you are Real, your hair has fallen off, your eyes are lost, and you look very old and shabby."

"Are you Real?" asked the rabbit.

"Oh, yes," said the horse. "Matt's father made me Real many years ago when he was still a boy. Once you are Real, it lasts forever." The rabbit wished he could be as Real as the horse.

(1) Is 'Real' about how you are made or what happens to you?
'Real' is what _____.

(2) Does 'Real' happen all at once or bit by bit?
'Real' happens _____.

(3) Can any toy become 'Real?'
It _____ to toys that break easily.

(4) When you are 'Real,' do you look new and shiny or old?
When you are 'Real,' you look very _____ and _____.

(5) When did Matt's father make the horse real?
Matt's father made the horse real when he was _____.

You are reading really well!

Reading Comprehension
The Velveteen Rabbit 2

Level ★★★

Score

/100

34

Date   /   /

Name

1 Read the passage. Then answer the questions using words from the passage.

8 points per question

> For a while, the rabbit was lonely. Matt slept with his teddy bear all the time.
>
> Then one day, Matt lost his teddy bear. "Here," said the babysitter. "Take this fuzzy old bunny to help you sleep."
>
> From then on, the rabbit slept in the little boy's bed. At night, Matt made a tunnel under the sheets for the rabbit to sleep in. When the boy fell asleep, the rabbit slept under his chin.
>
> The rabbit had dreams of being Real while he slept in the boy's arms all night long.
>
> The months passed, and the little rabbit was happy. He was so happy that he did not see how his coat got worn off. He did not see that his spots faded and his smooth pink ears turned gray and bumpy. He did not see that the pink on his nose rubbed off where the boy had kissed him.

(1) What did Matt lose?
Matt lost his favorite _____.

(2) Where did Matt make a tunnel for the rabbit?
Matt made a tunnel _____ the _____.

(3) When would the rabbit sleep under the boy's chin?
The rabbit slept under his chin when the _____.

(4) How did the little rabbit feel for months?
For months, the little rabbit was _____.

(5) Did his spots get bright or fade?
The rabbit's spots _____.

2 Read the passage. Then answer the questions using words from the passage.

12 points per question

Then that fall, the boy became ill. For a long time, the boy was too sick to play. The rabbit hugged him while he was asleep. "Get better soon," the rabbit sang.

When the boy got better, all the old toys had to be thrown out. The rabbit went into the trash with some sheets and books and old cans.

The rabbit cried a real tear. Then his nose twitched. His legs moved. At last, he became Real. He could leap for joy, which he did. In spring, when the days grew warm and sunny, the rabbit looked for the boy. When the rabbit found the boy, the boy said, "He looks just like my old Bunny." Happy to see their old friend, they both smiled.

(1) For how long was the boy sick?
The boy was sick for a _____.

(2) When did the old toys have to be thrown out?
All the old toys had to be thrown out when the boy _____.

(3) Which happened first? Did the Rabbit move his legs first or did he cry a real tear first?
The rabbit _____ first.

(4) In spring, were the days warm and sunny or cold and rainy?
The days were _____.

(5) Why did the rabbit and boy smile?
They smiled because they were _____ each other.

You are a real reader!

© Kumon Publishing Co., Ltd. 69

Review

1 Complete each sentence using a word from the box.   2 points per question

strong   chin   whale   third   watch   mouse   right   throw

(1) A very big _____ swam by our boat.

(2) I am sad. I only came in _____ in the race.

(3) Some of your soup is on your _____.

(4) Will you _____ my dog for a little bit?

(5) Mom was very scared. She saw a _____.

(6) I picked up a big box. I am _____!

(7) We have to turn _____ at the light.

(8) Can you _____ me the ball?

2 Complete each sentence using a word from the box.   3 points per question

price   potatoes   point   hammer   carrot   night   stories   cowboy

(1) I need a _____ for this nail.

(2) The _____ for these apples is too high!

(3) Ben always has a light on at _____.

(4) You have to boil the _____ to get them soft.

(5) I am hungry. I would like a _____.

(6) It is rude to _____ at a person.

(7) Tony wants to be a _____ when he grows up.

(8) My father likes to tell long _____.

3 Draw a line between the two words that mean the **opposite**.

5 points per question

(1) up •   • ⓐ right

(2) left •   • ⓑ down

(3) in •   • ⓒ out

(4) over •   • ⓓ slow

(5) hot •   • ⓔ under

(6) fast •   • ⓕ cold

4 Complete the charts below.

5 points per question

One	More than one
apple	(1)
(2)	benches
match	(3)

One	More than one
(4)	frogs
story	(5)
(6)	bushes

Review
Playing Sports / Texas

36

Level
☆☆

Score

Date   /   /

Name

/100

1 Read the following passage. Then answer the questions using words from the passage.

8 points per question

Playing Sports

Jin loves sports. No matter what the season, he is always playing a sport. Sometimes, he plays two! This summer, Jin went to soccer camp. For two weeks, all he did was eat, sleep, and play soccer. After soccer camp, he also went to basketball camp. His summer was fun.

Jin plays soccer in the fall also. He can't decide which sport he likes best. He plays soccer the most. Jin is fast, and often he can run by the other team and score goals. Late in the fall, he plays some basketball, too. He needs to be ready for basketball season in the winter.

He plays only basketball all winter because they play a lot of games. The day after basketball season ends, he has to go to his first spring baseball game! Jin is always playing a sport.

(1) Where did Jin go this summer?

Jin went to _____ and _____ camp this summer.

(2) Which sport does Jin like best?

Jin can't _____ which sport he likes best.

(3) Why does Jin play only basketball in the winter?

Jin plays only basketball in the winter because they play a lot of

_____.

(4) When does he have his first spring baseball game?

Jin has his first spring baseball game the _____ basketball season ends.

(5) What is Jin always doing?

Jin is always _____.

2 Read the passage. Then answer the questions using words from the passage.

Texas

Texas is a big state. It has many cows and cowboys. It has lots of dust as well. It has lots of everything, because it is so big!

Texas cowboys dress well for the jobs they do. They wear extra strong pants and jackets. They have nice, strong boots. Their big hats block the sun.

Much of Texas is flat grassland. It also has hills, cliffs, and beaches. Most of the time, it is very hot. The state often has big thunderstorms also.

If you go on a trip to Texas, it will help if you have a big map. The state is over 770 miles wide and 790 miles long! In America, only one state is bigger than Texas.

(1) What kind of a state is Texas?

Texas is a _____ state.

(2) Who wears nice strong boots in Texas?

Texas _____ _____ wear nice strong boots and dress well.

(3) What sort of storms does Texas often have?

Texas has big _____.

(4) What will help you if you go on a trip to Texas?

It will help if you have a _____.

(5) How many states are bigger than Texas?

Only _____ state is bigger than Texas.

Wow. You did it! Well done!

1 Vocabulary Review pp 2,3

1 (1) block (2) clap
(3) flag (4) plug
(5) frog

2 (1) grass (2) play
(3) brag (4) crab
(5) fly (6) class

3 (1) ⓒ (2) ⓕ
(3) ⓑ (4) ⓔ
(5) ⓓ (6) ⓐ

4 (1) flag (2) class
(3) grass (4) block
(5) plum (6) clock

2 Vocabulary Review pp 4,5

1 (1) ⓔ (2) ⓕ
(3) ⓓ (4) ⓑ
(5) ⓐ (6) ⓒ

2 (1) skate (2) snap
(3) slip (4) class
(5) slide (6) glove

3 (1) tent (2) wind
(3) stamp (4) lamp
(5) drink (6) plant
(7) test (8) lick

4 (1) pink (2) lost
(3) end (4) rock

3 Vocabulary Review pp 6,7

1 (1) street (2) string
(3) stripe (4) stream
(5) splash (6) spray
(7) strong (8) split

2 (1) ⓑ (2) ⓐ
(3) ⓐ (4) ⓑ
(5) ⓑ (6) ⓐ

3 (1) pretty (2) print
(3) stick (4) stop
(5) string (6) star
(7) spoon (8) spot

4 (1) splash (2) stream
(3) street (4) spray
(5) strong

4 Vocabulary Review pp 8,9

1 (1) stretch (2) scratch
(3) watch (4) father
(5) cloth (6) witch
(7) three (8) mother

2 (1) brother (2) witch
(3) stretch (4) catch

3 (1) witch (2) watch
(3) mother (4) cloth
(5) catch (6) stretch

4 (1) father (2) watch
(3) scratch (4) three
(5) stretch

5　Vowels

pp 10, 11

1　(1) car　　(2) first

(3) fur　　(4) her

(5) horn　　(6) hard

(7) jar　　(8) bird

(9) cart　　(10) fork

2　(1) ⓗ / ⓓ　　(2) ⓒ / ⓖ

(3) ⓕ / ⓛ　　(4) ⓔ / ⓙ

(5) ⓚ / ⓐ　　(6) ⓑ / ⓘ

3　(1) jar　　(2) fork

(3) fur　　(4) cart

(5) bird　　(6) horn

4　(1) jar　　(2) bird

(3) horn　　(4) fork

(5) fur　　(6) first

6　Vowels

pp 12, 13

1　(1) coin　　(2) boy

(3) point　　(4) soil

(5) toy　　(6) enjoy

2　(1) ⓐ　　(2) ⓑ

(3) ⓐ　　(4) ⓑ

(5) ⓑ　　(6) ⓐ

3　(1) joy　　(2) toy

(3) point　　(4) soil

(5) boil　　(6) coin

(7) boy　　(8) join

4　(1) point　　(2) boil

(3) coin　　(4) toy

(5) enjoy

7　Vowels

pp 14, 15

1　(1) cloud　　(2) house

(3) mouth　　(4) loud

(5) out　　(6) round

(7) mouse

2　(1) you　　(2) soup

(3) group

3　(1) ⓑ　　(2) ⓓ

(3) ⓐ　　(4) ⓒ

4　(1) throw　　(2) crow

(3) arrow　　(4) bow

(5) tower　　(6) cow

(7) down　　(8) flower

5　(1) tower　　(2) round

(3) cow　　(4) arrow

(5) flower　　(6) crow

8　Vowels

pp 16, 17

1　(1) room　　(2) tooth

(3) stool　　(4) broom

(5) moon　　(6) pool

(7) boot　　(8) spoon

2　(1) ⓓ　　(2) ⓖ

(3) ⓑ　　(4) ⓕ

(5) ⓔ　　(6) ⓗ

(7) ⓐ　　(8) ⓒ

3　(1) foot　　(2) look

(3) hook　　(4) wood

(5) good　　(6) took

(7) book　　(8) cook

4 (1) book (2) pool
(3) foot (4) spoon
(5) room (6) look

9 Vowels

pp 18,19

1 (1) nice (2) dice
(3) mice (4) ice
(5) price (6) rice

2 (1) ⓑ (2) ⓐ
(3) ⓐ (4) ⓐ

3 (1) flight (2) bright
(3) right (4) fright
(5) light (6) night
(7) sight

4 (1) right (2) ice
(3) light (4) night
(5) mice (6) nice

10 Consonant Combinations

pp 20,21

1 (1) ball (2) doll
(3) fall (4) bull
(5) spill (6) smell
(7) tall (8) spell

2 (1) off (2) boss
(3) class (4) kiss
(5) press (6) sniff
(7) grass (8) cliff

3 (1) ball / balloon (2) bell / belly
(3) bull / bully (4) yell / yellow
(5) off / offer

4 (1) class (2) ball
(3) sniff (4) off
(5) offer (6) balloon

11 Consonant Combinations

pp 22,23

1 (1) summer (2) hurry
(3) tunnel (4) winner
(5) mirror (6) hammer
(7) carrot (8) parrot

2 (1) ⓐ (2) ⓕ
(3) ⓓ (4) ⓗ
(5) ⓑ (6) ⓔ
(7) ⓖ (8) ⓒ

3 (1) carrot (2) summer
(3) tunnel (4) dinner
(5) berry (6) yellow
(7) hello (8) funny

4 (1) summer (2) parrot
(3) hurry (4) winner
(5) jelly (6) mirror

12 Compound Words

pp 24,25

1 (1) snowman (2) uphill
(3) blackbird

2 (1) ①ⓗ ②ⓐ ③ⓙ
(2) ①ⓖ ②ⓑ ③ⓔ
(3) ①ⓞ ②ⓚ ③ⓒ
(4) ①ⓛ ②ⓓ ③ⓕ
(5) ①ⓝ ②ⓘ ③ⓜ

3 (1) upstairs (2) snowflake
(3) cowboy (4) fireplace
(5) grasshopper (6) rainbow

4 (1) shoemaker   (2) playground
     (3) lunchroom   (4) fireplace
     (5) football   (6) cowboy

13 **Compound Words**   pp 26, 27

1 (1) <u>snowman</u> / snow / man
    (2) <u>fireplace</u> / fire / place
    (3) <u>uphill</u> / up / hill
    (4) <u>notebook</u> / note / book
    (5) <u>sandcastle</u> / sand / castle

2 birthday / uphill / playground /
   blueberry / football / rainbow

3 baseball / grandfather / grandmother /
   lightbulb / moonlight / snowshoe /
   snowball / snowflake / sunlight

4 (1) notebook   (2) snowball
    (3) birthday   (4) downstairs
    (5) bluebird

14 **Synonyms**   pp 28, 29

1 (1) icy   (2) large
    (3) sturdy   (4) rosy
    (5) small

2 (1) ⓑ   (2) ⓐ
    (3) ⓖ   (4) ⓒ
    (5) ⓓ   (6) ⓕ
    (7) ⓔ

3 (1) pull   (2) lift
    (3) shake   (4) house
    (5) seat   (6) road
    (7) close

4 (1) ⓑ   (2) ⓐ
    (3) ⓒ

15 **Antonyms**   pp 30, 31

1 (1) ⓒ   (2) ⓓ
    (3) ⓔ   (4) ⓙ
    (5) ⓖ   (6) ⓗ
    (7) ⓘ   (8) ⓕ
    (9) ⓐ   (10) ⓑ

2 (1) up   (2) down
    (3) over   (4) under
    (5) top   (6) bottom
    (7) near   (8) far

3 (1) ⓒ   (2) ⓐ
    (3) ⓓ   (4) ⓑ
    (5) ⓔ

4 (1) outside   (2) left
    (3) unhappy   (4) loud
    (5) slow   (6) downstairs

16 **Synonyms & Antonyms**   pp 32, 33

1 (1) loud   (2) little
    (3) cold   (4) joyful
    (5) sad   (6) wet

2 (1) O   (2) O
    (3) S   (4) S
    (5) O

3 (1) nighttime   (2) asleep
    (3) few   (4) empty
    (5) never   (6) huge

4

(17) Synonyms & Antonyms
pp 34,35

1 (1) away   (2) finish
    (3) scary   (4) hard
    (5) heavy

2 (1) O   (2) O
    (3) O   (4) O
    (5) S

3 (1) ⓒ   (2) ⓔ
    (3) ⓓ   (4) ⓑ
    (5) ⓐ

4 (1) huge   (2) full
    (3) friendly   (4) most
    (5) never

(18) Irregular Plurals
pp 36,37

1 (1) bushes   (2) benches
    (3) dishes   (4) tomatoes
    (5) babies   (6) stories
    (7) candies   (8) bunnies

2 (1) dishes   (2) cities
    (3) churches   (4) potatoes
    (5) ladies   (6) candies

3 (1) wishes   (2) bench
    (3) matches   (4) potato
    (5) baby   (6) stories
    (7) candy   (8) families

4 (1) watch   (2) baby
    (3) benches   (4) stories
    (5) tomatoes   (6) party
    (7) brushes   (8) beach

(19) Who / When / Where
pp 38,39

1 (1) New York   (2) time ago
2 (1) throws   (2) bats
    (3) score
3 (1) three strikes   (2) three outs
4 (1) out   (2) 60

(20) Who / When / Where
pp 40,41

1 (1) baseball   (2) a train
2 (1) crowd   (2) team
    (3) game
3 (1) ball game   (2) three
    (3) peanuts / cracker
4 (1) popcorn   (2) baseball
    (3) peanuts   (4) strikes

(21) What / Why
pp 42,43

1 (1) windstorm   (2) snow / ice
    (3) snowstorm   (4) safe place
    (5) snowdrift
2 (1) pool of water   (2) fill up / spill
    (3) few inches / high
    (4) lights go out
    (5) clean water

(22) What / Why
pp 44,45

1 (1) balls / card   (2) pet rock
    (3) umbrella   (4) sunny / hot
    (5) edge / sandcastle
2 (1) water / close   (2) jumps / splashes
    (3) apples / grapes   (4) new pet rock
    (5) towel

23 Who / What / When / Where / Why pp 46,47

1 (1) once upon (2) beach
(3) other places (4) two frogs
(5) stopped

2 (1) taller (2) held / up
(3) eyes / tops / heads (4) own city
(5) looked the same

24 Who / What / When / Where / Why pp 48,49

1 (1) Bees (2) Pollen
(3) for food (4) flower
(5) grow

2 (1) uncle (Stan) (2) comic book
(3) walls / room (4) after school
(5) good title

25 Reading the Table of Contents pp 50,51

1 (1) Flea / Hole (2) 2
(3) Frog / Walk (4) 24
(5) Yes

2 (1) Sunny Day (2) 5
(3) 16 (4) The Kite is Stuck
(5) 32

26 Sequence pp 52,53

1 (1) 1 (2) 6
(3) 2 (4) 5
(5) 4 (6) 3

2 (1) 8 (2) 1
(3) 5 (4) 3
(5) 4 (6) 6
(7) 2 (8) 7

27 Reading Comprehension pp 54,55

1 (1) home [nest] (2) singing
(3) work (4) winter
(5) No / resting

2 (1) plenty / food (2) winter
(3) stored (4) help / worked
(5) good / save

28 Reading Comprehension pp 56,57

1 (1) more friends
(2) looking / walking
(3) swim very well
(4) dove (5) leaf / river

2 (1) fuss (2) net / hands
(3) trying / catch (4) sunk / teeth
(5) good friend

29 Reading Comprehension pp 58,59

1 (1) dog (2) child
(3) nice / learn (4) snacks
(5) shares

2 (1) chin (2) throws the stick
(3) brings / stick (4) over and over
(5) doesn't throw

30 Reading Comprehension pp 60,61

1 (1) walk (2) leash / collar
(3) her hand (4) hard time
(5) will get hurt

2 (1) too fast (2) falls down
(3) feel better (4) the dog / child
(5) soft bark

31 Reading Comprehension pp 62,63

1 (1) poor   (2) hid
   (3) came / away   (4) robber / take
   (5) waved

2 (1) 1   (2) 7
   (3) 5   (4) 8
   (5) 3   (6) 4
   (7) 2   (8) 6

32 Reading Comprehension pp 64,65

1 (1) ran home   (2) share
   (3) little   (4) old
   (5) boiled full

2 (1) enough / for all   (2) dishes
   (3) poor / good food   (4) a stone
   (5) little girl / family

33 Reading Comprehension pp 66,67

1 (1) birthday   (2) whole hour
   (3) high shelf   (4) father
   (5) horse

2 (1) happens to you
   (2) bit by bit   (3) does not happen
   (4) old / shabby   (5) still a boy

34 Reading Comprehension pp 68,69

1 (1) teddy bear   (2) under / sheets
   (3) boy fell asleep
   (4) happy   (5) faded

2 (1) long time   (2) got better
   (3) cried a real tear (4) warm and sunny
   (5) happy to see

35 Review pp 70,71

1 (1) whale   (2) third
   (3) chin   (4) watch
   (5) mouse   (6) strong
   (7) right   (8) throw

2 (1) hammer   (2) price
   (3) night   (4) potatoes
   (5) carrot   (6) point
   (7) cowboy   (8) stories

3 (1) ⓑ   (2) ⓐ
   (3) ⓒ   (4) ⓔ
   (5) ⓕ   (6) ⓓ

4 (1) apples   (2) bench
   (3) matches   (4) frog
   (5) stories   (6) bush

36 Review pp 72,73

1 (1) soccer / basketball   (2) decide
   (3) games   (4) day after
   (5) playing a sport

2 (1) big   (2) cowboys
   (3) thunderstorms (4) big map
   (5) one